WINTER OLYMPIC SPORTS

ALPINE AND FREESTYLE SKIING

by Kylie Burns

Words that are defined in the glossary are in **bold** type the first time they appear in the text.

A table of abbreviations used for the names of countries appears on page 32.

Crabtree editor: Adrianna Morganelli
Proofreader: Crystal Sikkens
Editorial director: Kathy Middleton
Production coordinator and
  prepress technician: Katherine Berti
Developed for Crabtree Publishing Company by
RJF Publishing LLC (www.RJFpublishing.com)
Editor: Jacqueline Laks Gorman
Designer: Tammy West, Westgraphix LLC
Photo Researcher: Edward A. Thomas
Indexer: Nila Glikin

Photo Credits:
Alamy: INTERFOTO Pressebildagentur: p. 10
Corbis: Dimitri Iundt/TempSport: p. 19; Jerome Prevost/
  TempSport: p. 13; Jonathan Selkowitz/NewSport: p. 28
Getty Images: p. 2, 7, 12, 16, 18, 20, 22, 23; AFP: p. 8, 15,
  19, 25; Bongarts: p. 24; Sports Illustrated: p. 4, 6, 14
Landov: Eric Gaillard/Reuters: front cover; Kyodo: p. 26
Wikipedia: Arnold C (Buchanan-Hermit): p. 29

Cover: Jennifer Heil of Canada in moguls competition at
the 2006 Winter Olympics.

CONTENTS

Library and Archives Canada Cataloguing in Publication

Burns, Kylie
    Alpine and freestyle skiing / Kylie Burns.

(Winter Olympic sports)
Includes index.
ISBN 978-0-7787-4020-9 (bound).--ISBN 978-0-7787-4039-1 (pbk.)

    1. Downhill skiing--Juvenile literature. 2. Freestyle skiing--
Juvenile literature. 3. Winter Olympics--Juvenile literature. I. Title.
II. Series: Winter Olympic sports

GV854.315.B87 2009   j796.93'5   C2009-903208-2

Library of Congress Cataloging-in-Publication Data

Burns, Kylie.
    Alpine and freestyle skiing / Kylie Burns.
        p. cm. -- (Winter Olympic sports)
    Includes index.
    ISBN 978-0-7787-4039-1 (pbk. : alk. paper) -- ISBN 978-0-7787-
4020-9 (reinforced library binding : alk. paper)
    1. Downhill skiing. 2. Freestyle skiing. 3. Skis and skiing. I.
Title.

    GV854.B87 2010
    796.93'5--dc22
                                                    2009021487

Crabtree Publishing Company

www.crabtreebooks.com   1-800-387-7650
Copyright © 2010 CRABTREE PUBLISHING COMPANY. All rights reserved. No part of this publication may be reproduced, stored in a retrieval system or be transmitted in any form or by any means, electronic, mechanical, photocopying, recording, or otherwise, without the prior written permission of Crabtree Publishing Company. In Canada: We acknowledge the financial support of the Government of Canada through the Book Publishing Industry Development Program (BPIDP) for our publishing activities.

Published in Canada	Published in the United States	Published in the United Kingdom	Published in Australia
Crabtree Publishing	Crabtree Publishing	Crabtree Publishing	Crabtree Publishing
616 Welland Ave.	PMB16A	White Cross Mills	386 Mt. Alexander Rd.
St. Catharines, ON	350 Fifth Ave., Suite 3308	High Town, Lancaster	Ascot Vale (Melbourne)
L2M 5V6	New York, NY 10118	LA1 4XS	VIC 3032

OLYMPIC SKIING EVENTS

In the Winter Olympics, alpine and freestyle skiing are all about speed, skill, and excitement!

Julia Mancuso (USA) skis for gold in the women's giant slalom at the 2006 Winter Olympics.

ALPINE AND FREESTYLE SKIING

Alpine skiing involves five types of races—downhill, slalom, giant slalom, Super-G, and super combined—in which skiers speed down the hill. In freestyle skiing, competitors ski down the hill as well, but with tricks and acrobatics thrown in.

ANCIENT AND NEWER ORIGINS

People have been practicing alpine skiing in the Alps of Europe for at least 150 years. Freestyle skiing is a much newer sport, developed in the 1960s. The first Olympic skiing event took place in 1936, with an event called the alpine combined. Freestyle did not enter the Olympics until 1992.

EQUALITY OF THE SEXES

Men and women compete in all of the alpine and freestyle events.

SWITCHING SKIS

Daron Rahlves (USA) was an expert downhill skier who won many medals in international competition. He retired from the U.S. alpine ski team in 2006, after 13 years, and decided to switch to freestyle skiing. Now, he competes in the newer sport of ski cross.

OLYMPICS FACT FILE

- The Olympic Games were first held in Olympia, in ancient Greece, around 3,000 years ago. They took place every four years until they were abolished in 393 A.D. A Frenchman named Pierre Coubertin (1863–1937) revived the Games, and the first modern Olympics—which featured only summer sports—were held in Athens in 1896.

- The first Olympic Winter Games were held in 1924 in Chamonix, France. The Winter Games were then held every four years except in 1940 and 1944 (because of World War II), taking place in the same year as the Summer Games, until 1992.

- The International Olympic Committee decided to stage the Summer and Winter Games in different years, so there was only a two-year gap before the next Winter Games were held in 1994. They have been held every four years from that time.

- The symbol of the Olympic Games is five interlocking colored rings. Together, they represent the union of the five regions of the world—Africa, the Americas, Asia, Europe, and Oceania (Australia and the Pacific Islands)—as athletes come together to compete in the Games.

INTRODUCTION TO ALPINE SKIING

Skiers competing in alpine events make a series of turns while
racing down the hill at speeds of more than 81 MPH (130 km/h).
Their goal—to get to the finish line the fastest!

Norway's Kjetil André Aamodt in
action on the Super-G course in 2006.

Austrian alpine skiers have won more medals at the Winter Olympics than any other country with a combined total of 101—including 30 golds!

ON THE RUN

Alpine skiing events at the Vancouver 2010 Olympics will be held at Whistler Creekside, on the Dave Murray Downhill for men's events and Franz's Run for women's races.

TRIPLE THREAT

A Triple Crown champion is an athlete who wins gold medals during the same Olympics for three of the alpine events—slalom, giant slalom, and downhill. Only two men have done this—Toni Sailer (AUT) in 1956 and Jean-Claude Killy (FRA) in 1968. No woman has won a Triple Crown, but Rosi Mittermaier (FRG) came close in 1976. She won gold in the downhill and slalom and just lost the giant slalom by only twelve-hundredths of a second!

POLAR OPPOSITES

The term *poles* refers to both the equipment skiers use to thrust forward, turn, and land during competition and the posts that are planted firmly into the snow along a race course.

CRASH!

Crashes and falls are common in downhill and Super-G, which are very fast races. Crashes are rare in slalom and giant slalom, but those events often see skiers falling and making errors along the course.

DID YOU KNOW?

• Skis were originally carved completely from wood. In 1928, steel edges were added to make turning easier. The steel edges were fastened with screws that sometimes fell out, so skiers had to be sure to carry a screwdriver and extra screws!

• Today, most skis are made from a combination of materials including wood, plastic, fiberglass, graphite, aluminum, and steel.

HIS AND HERS

Kjetil André Aamodt (NOR) holds the record for the most Olympic medals in alpine skiing, with eight. Janica Kostelić (CRO) holds the woman's record of six.

SETTLING LIMITS

Nations are given limits on the number of skiers they can enter in the alpine events at the Olympics. Each country may enter up to 22 skiers. In addition, each country may have no more than four skiers in any separate alpine event.

DOWNHILL

Downhill skiing was officially added to the Olympics in 1948.

Scott Macartney (USA) in the starting gate at the beginning of the 2006 downhill race.

PERFECT TIMING

A downhill competitor begins the race at a starting gate when he hears a series of 10 electronic beeps. As soon as he pushes the gate open, an electronic timer begins. When he crosses the finish line, an infrared beam is interrupted, stopping the timer. The time is recorded to the nearest hundredth of a second. Ties are possible, but very rare.

2006 OLYMPIC MEDALISTS: MEN: GOLD: ANTOINE DÉNÉRIAZ (FRA)
SILVER: MICHAEL WALCHHOFER (AUT)   BRONZE: BRUNO KERNEN (SUI)

DID YOU KNOW?
- In 1948, during the **debut** of downhill competition, two athletes from Switzerland tied for the bronze medal with identical times of 3:00.3.

- The first skier to win the downhill event twice was Katja Seizinger (GER), who captured the gold in both 1994 and 1998.

RACE BASICS

Downhill races require high-speed skiing combined with precise turns. Skiers weave through a series of gates on the course during a single run. This is the longest alpine race, with the highest speeds.

BREAKAWAY

Before the 1980s, gates were made of hard, inflexible bamboo. Today's gates — called **breakaway gates** — are made from plastic with **hinges** that allow the gates to bend and snap back into position after a skier zooms by.

DISQUALIFIED!

An athlete must ski between all of the gates on the course. If she misses a gate, she must go back uphill and ski it correctly. Otherwise, she will be **disqualified** from the race.

Michaela Dorfmeister (AUT) won two gold medals in alpine skiing in 2006.

FIGHT TO THE FINISH

In the 1976 Olympic men's downhill race, Franz Klammer (AUT) realized he was not skiing fast enough to win. He quickly fought back in the last stretch of the race and won gold by 0.33 seconds!

SLALOM

Slalom is the shortest, fastest race in alpine skiing. Slalom was introduced to the Olympics in 1948 and has been part of every Winter Olympics since then.

The men's medalists—all from Austria—celebrate a sweep of the 2006 Olympic slalom event.

2006 OLYMPIC MEDALISTS: MEN: GOLD: BENJAMIN RAICH (AUT)
SILVER: REINFRIED HERBST (AUT)   BRONZE: RAINER SCHÖNFELDER (AUT)

When Benjamin Raich (AUT) won the men's slalom at the 2006 Olympics, he skied the first run in 53.37 seconds and the second in 49.77 seconds, for a total time of 1:43.14. The women's winner, Anja Pärson (SWE), posted times of 42.38 seconds and 46.66 seconds, for a total time of 1:29.04.

DID YOU KNOW?

At the 1952 Games, one competitor crossed the finish line in the slalom backward! Antoin Miliordos (GRE) did just that after he got angry because he fell 18 times. His time for one run was almost a half-minute slower than the time posted by the winner—Othmar Schneider (AUT)—for two runs.

RACE BASICS

Each competitor races down two different courses on the same day. The times for both races are added together, and the fastest total time wins. There are between 55 and 75 gates in men's slalom and between 40 and 60 gates in women's slalom. The gates are placed close together, which forces skiers to make quick, sharp turns. A skier's feet and ski tips must pass between red and blue poles for each gate. If a skier misses a gate, she is disqualified.

ALL IN THE FAMILY

During the 1960s, sisters Marielle and Christine Goitschel (FRA) were among the world's best female skiers. In the 1964 Olympics, they dominated the **podium** in slalom and giant slalom. That year, Christine won gold in slalom, and Marielle took silver. The roles were reversed for giant slalom—Marielle won gold, and Christine won silver!

GIRL POWER

The first U.S. skier to win an Olympic gold medal was Gretchen Fraser in 1948, when she captured gold in slalom. The first Canadian alpine champion was Anne Heggtveit, who won the slalom in 1960.

SUPERMEN

Benjamin Raich (AUT) won both the slalom and giant slalom in 2006. In slalom, his Austrian teammates won silver and bronze.

FIRST MEDAL WINNERS

In 1948, when the slalom was first contested at the Winter Olympics, Edi Reinalter (SUI) won the first men's gold medal. Gretchen Fraser (USA) won the first women's gold medal.

COMEBACK

Andrea Mead Lawrence (USA) won the giant slalom at the 1952 Winter Olympics, but a few days later, she fell in the first run of the slalom. She got up and managed to finish the run in fourth place. Then she was perfect in the second run, skiing two seconds faster than any of her competitors. She became the first American to win two golds in alpine skiing.

GIANT SLALOM

With high speeds and fast turns, giant slalom is widely regarded as the most physically demanding event in alpine skiing.

Alberto Tomba (ITA), one of the greatest slalom and giant slalom skiers ever, in action in 1998.

goggles

ski poles

knee pads

skis

shin pads

2006 OLYMPIC MEDALISTS: MEN: GOLD: BENJAMIN RAICH (AUT)
SILVER: JOËL CHENAL (FRA)   BRONZE: HERMANN MAIER (AUT)

RACE BASICS

The giant slalom is very similar to slalom except that the course is longer. Athletes perform two runs on the same day, down the same slope, but on different courses. The results from each run are added together to determine the fastest time. Giant slalom made its debut as an Olympic sport in 1948.

GEARING UP

Alpine skiers need clothing that is tight-fitting and **aerodynamic**. For protection, they now must wear crash helmets. They also wear goggles, heavy ski gloves, and padding on their knees, arms, and shins.

EARLY START

Ingemar Stenmark (SWE) started skiing at the age of five. By the time he was eight years old, he already had a national championship under his belt! In 1980, he won gold medals in both the slalom and giant slalom.

SEE YOU LATER!

In 1956, Toni Sailer (AUT) won gold in the giant slalom way ahead of the silver medalist—a staggering 6.2 seconds! This is the largest **margin of victory** in Olympic alpine skiing history.

DID YOU KNOW?

Only hundredths of a second separated the men's medalists in the 2006 giant slalom. Benjamin Raich (AUT), the gold medal winner, posted a time of 2:35.00. The silver medalist, Jöel Chenal (FRA), finished in 2:35.07, and the bronze medalist, Hermann Maier (AUT), had a time of 2:35.16.

QUEEN OF THE MOUNTAIN

Julia Mancuso (USA) skied to victory in the women's giant slalom in 2006 with a time of 2:09.19. She had worn a plastic **tiara** in races as a good luck charm since 2005, but she took it off for the Olympics. She still had good luck!

DYNAMITE!

Alberto Tomba (ITA) became the first skier to win an Olympic event twice when he won the giant slalom in 1988 and 1992. He is also the first athlete in Olympic history to win medals in three separate Olympics. No wonder they call him "Tomba La Bomba"!

CANADA'S STAR

Nancy Greene (CAN) won the giant slalom at the 1968 Olympics by a whopping 2.64 seconds! She also won silver for slalom, making her the first Canadian to win two medals in the Olympics. She was named "Canada's Female Athlete of the Century" in 1999.

SUPER-G

One of the youngest alpine events, Super-G (for super giant slalom) became an Olympic sport in 1988.

Italy's Deborah Compagnoni, winning the Super-G in 1992.

2006 OLYMPIC MEDALISTS: MEN:
SILVER: HERMANN MAIER (AUT)
GOLD: KJETIL ANDRÉ AAMODT (NOR)
BRONZE: AMBROSI HOFFMANN (SUI)

RACE BASICS

Super-G has fewer gates on a longer course than giant slalom, combining the speed of downhill racing with technical slalom skills. Competitors ski only once, and the fastest time wins.

"THE HERMANNATOR"

Hermann Maier (AUT), one of the most famous Super-G skiers in history, is known for being fearless. He experienced a terrible crash in the 1998 Olympics when he slipped on an icy turn during the downhill race. Amazingly, he went on to win gold medals in the Super-G and giant slalom just a few days later!

SNOW BIZ

Snow conditions affect a ski racer's speed and turns and even the selection of skis for a race. Some snow conditions are ideal for racing, and some are downright dangerous! For racing, most skiers prefer packed powder—natural or man-made snow that has been **compacted** by skiers or grooming machines.

DID YOU KNOW?

Super-G and downhill ski poles are curved to fit around the body, which reduces **wind resistance**. Slalom and giant slalom poles, on the other hand, are straight.

TRIPLE PLAY

Deborah Compagnoni (ITA) achieved something no other alpine skier had done before—she became the first skier to win gold in three different Olympics. She won the Super-G in 1992 and two giant slalom competitions in 1994 and 1998.

DOUBLE DUTY

Michaela Dorfmeister (AUT) won both the women's Super-G and downhill at the 2006 Olympics, becoming the first woman to win both events at the same Games.

Austria's Hermann Maier crosses the finish line in triumph in the 1998 Super-G.

2006 OLYMPIC MEDALISTS: WOMEN:
SILVER: JANICA KOSTELIĆ (CRO)

GOLD: MICHAELA DORFMEISTER (AUT)
BRONZE: ALEXANDRA MEISSNITZER (AUT)

SUPER COMBINED

The super combined mixes two contests—downhill and slalom—to test athletes' speed and technical skill.

Ted Ligety (USA) on the slopes during the slalom portion of the 2006 super combined.

2006 OLYMPIC MEDALISTS: MEN:　　GOLD: TED LIGETY (USA)
SILVER: IVICA KOSTELIĆ (CRO)　　BRONZE: RAINER SCHÖNFELDER (AUT)

OLYMPIC HISTORY

The combined event was first included in the 1936 Olympics as the alpine combined, which consisted of one downhill run and two slalom runs. The alpine combined appeared again in 1948. Then the event disappeared until 1988, when it surfaced under the name super combined.

RACE BASICS

From 1998 through 2006, competitors in the combined raced three times over two days, doing one downhill run plus two slalom runs. At the 2010 Olympics, the super combined will consist of one downhill run and one slalom run, both done on the same day. The winner is the athlete with the fastest total time.

LIGETY-SPLIT!

Ted Ligety (USA) won gold in the combined event at the 2006 Olympics. It was his first Olympic win — and his first time at the Olympics!

Brother and sister Ivica and Janica Kostelić (CRO) celebrate their medals in the super combined.

CRASH LANDING

Filip Trejbal (CZE) learned the hard way that skiing is a dangerous sport. During the downhill portion of the super combined at the 2006 Olympics, the skier lost his balance. His helmet flew off and he bounced helplessly over the snow until he finally skidded to a stop. He was carried off on a stretcher and taken to a nearby hospital. Remarkably, he survived the crash with no more than a few scrapes and bruises!

DID YOU KNOW?

Since the winner of the super combined is determined by adding the scores of the downhill run and the slalom run, the winner is not necessarily the skier who goes the fastest in either of the runs.

FAMILY TIES

The gold medalist at the 2006 Olympics in the women's combined event was Janica Kostelić (CRO). Her brother, Ivica Kostelić (CRO), won silver in the men's combined at the same Olympic Games!

INTRODUCTION TO FREESTYLE SKIING

If you like fast skiing and thrilling midair acrobatic moves, then you'll love freestyle skiing!

An amazing aerials move by Dmitri Rak (BLR).

A YOUNG HISTORY

Olympic freestyle skiing includes three events—aerials, moguls, and ski cross. The sport had its beginnings in the 1960s, when some alpine skiers began trying difficult midair tricks such as somersaults, fancy twists, and jumps. This style of skiing involves skill, athletic training, and a lot of courage!

IT'S FINAL!

Each freestyle event includes one or more **qualifying rounds** and a final round. The qualifying rounds determine which athletes perform well enough to compete in the final. The winner of the final gets the gold!

CARING CONSTRUCTION

All freestyle events at the 2010 Olympics will be held on Cypress Mountain, one of the most popular ski areas in the Vancouver area. Before the location was approved, an environmental review was done to make sure that plants and wildlife were protected. Some plants were carefully moved and planted in nearby wetlands when construction was done.

LET'S GET TRAINED

Training for freestyle skiing usually includes trampoline lessons, harness jumping, gymnastics, and over-water jumping practice. An athlete's body control is a key ingredient for performing midair jumps. Of course, freestyle skiers need to be skilled at basic alpine skiing, too.

DID YOU KNOW?

Ski ballet (also called acroski) was a **demonstration sport** for both men and women in the 1988 and 1992 Olympics. The event involved a 90-second sequence of acrobatic moves set to music. Ski ballet failed to become a full-fledged Olympic sport.

CANADIAN FIRST

Jean-Luc Brassard (CAN) became the first Canadian men's champion of a freestyle event in 1994 when he won the moguls competition.

Jean-Luc Brassard (CAN) winning the gold in men's moguls in 1994.

AERIALS

Aerials was a demonstration sport at the 1988 Olympics and was an instant hit with the crowd! It was officially added to the Winter Olympics in 1994.

Deidra Dionne (CAN) in action in the routine that won her a bronze medal in women's aerials at the 2002 Olympics.

BIG AIR

Competitors—who are known for taking big risks—perform two jumps of their choice in the qualifying round. The top 12 men and top 12 women move on to the final. Competitors are judged on quality of takeoff, jump height, form, and balanced landing. The winner is the athlete with the highest combined score after two jumps in the final round.

RULE BOOK

Scoring and judging aerials is an Olympic feat in itself! Judges include a **degree of difficulty** in each score. In other words, they must give higher scores to jumps involving harder, combined moves. Here is a breakdown of the scoring percentage for each jump: jump takeoff—20%, jump form—50%, landing—30%.

AWESOME AERIALS

The most difficult aerials moves involve combinations of twists, turns, and flips. The skier may hold the body straight, bent at the waist, or with the knees bent up. The skier may also launch into the jump by going backward or forward.

DOWNGRADED HURRICANE

In the finals of the 2006 Olympic aerials competition, Jeret "Speedy" Peterson (USA) made a risky decision when he chose to perform his famous "Hurricane" jump—three somersaults with five twists. He couldn't hold the landing, however, and finished in seventh place.

GREAT BEGINNINGS

Han Xiaopeng (CHN) was the youngest man to win the Olympic gold in aerials at age 22—and the first Chinese man to win a gold medal at a Winter Olympics!

Han Xiaopeng (CHN) executes a flip on the way to 2006 gold in men's aerials.

MORE ON AERIALS

Evelyne Leu (SUI) goes airborne to win the 2006 gold in women's aerials.

To perform high-flying aerial moves, athletes take off from a man-made kicker, or ramp. The height of the kicker depends on the number of somersaults a skier plans to perform.

FLIGHT PLAN

Athletes are required to file a plan for each of the two jumps they are going to perform. They must also indicate which of the three kickers they will use for each jump. If an athlete wishes to change a flight plan, she can — right up until just before she enters the start gate!

TRICKY TERMINOLOGY

Aerials moves have some complicated names. Some of them are called the Rudy, the Full Full Full, the Half Randy Full, and the Helicopter.

TWISTED MEDAL

Evelyne Leu (SUI) pushed herself to the limit at the 2006 Olympics when she successfully performed the hardest jump in the women's aerials event — a Full Full Full (involving three flips with three twists). Her hard work and determination paid off — she finished in first place!

RECORD BUT NO MEDAL

At the 2006 Olympics, Jacqui Cooper (AUS) set a women's world record of 213.56 points in the qualifying round of the aerials competition. In the finals, though, she missed the landings of both of her jumps and ended up in eighth place.

FIRST MEDALS

In 1994, the first men's Olympic gold medal ever awarded in aerials went to Andreas Schönbächler (SUI). Silver went to Philippe LaRoche (CAN) and bronze to Lloyd Langlois (CAN).

HIGH SCORES

When he won the gold medal in men's aerials at the 2006 Games, Han Xiaopeng (CHN) scored 250.77 points. The silver medalist, Dmitri Dashinski (BLR), recorded 248.68 points, and the bronze medalist, Vladimir Lebedev (RUS), had 246.76 points.

TRY, TRY AGAIN

In 1994 during training, Lina Cheryazova (UZB) crashed and was knocked unconscious. Later, during the qualifying round, she fell on her first jump. Her second qualifying jump scored well and earned her a spot in the finals. Amazingly, she won the gold medal by one full point!

NO PAIN, NO GAIN

Just before she was about to compete at the 2002 Olympics, Alisa Camplin (AUS) found out that a training injury she had suffered weeks earlier was in fact two fractured ankles. Against her doctor's orders, she skied in the women's aerials event anyway — and landed gracefully in first place with the gold medal!

MOGULS

If skiing at a high rate of speed down a snow-covered slope seems difficult enough, imagine the challenge of adding moguls, or large mounds of snow, to the race course!

Jonny Moseley (USA) performs his "Dinner Roll" in the men's moguls event in 2002.

OLYMPIC HISTORY

Moguls was the first freestyle skiing event in the Olympics, debuting in 1992.

LUMPS AND BUMPS

A mogul field is a ski hill with a lot of moguls, turns, grooves, and two **air bumps**. The air bumps are specially constructed jumps — one near the top of the run, and one near the bottom.

RACE BASICS

The steep course is about 820 feet (250 m) long. Athletes perform two different jumps of their choice during a single run, doing one jump on each air bump. Skiers are awarded points by judges based on speed, technique, and jump execution. The competitor with the highest score is the winner.

Australia's Dale Begg-Smith, on his way to gold in men's moguls in 2006.

TREND SETTER

Jean-Luc Brassard (CAN) was the first skier to use brightly colored knee pads in moguls competition. Judges noticed movement and turns more easily, which improved scoring accuracy. Now, colored knee pads are the standard among top moguls skiers!

MORE ON MOGULS

Kari Traa (NOR) in 1998, winning one of her three career medals in Olympic moguls competition.

Moguls competitors are scored for turns (worth 50%), air (25%), and speed (25%), with separate judges rating the different elements.

SUPER STATS

The United States has won the most medals in overall freestyle skiing at the Olympics, with 10. Canada, France, and Norway each have six overall medals.

MOVE IT!

In moguls competition, jumps are called *airs*. Airs can include grabs, holds, spins, and flips. Here are a few of the most common airs:

Back flip — a backward somersault

Twister — the upper body turns in the opposite direction that the skis turn

Daffy — one ski is in front, with ski tip pointing up, while the other ski is in back, with the tip pointing down

Spread eagle — arms and legs are extended out in the shape of an X

Mule kick — knees bent, legs together, kicking the skis up to one side

DID YOU KNOW?

• The first gold medal ever awarded in Olympic moguls competition went to Donna Weinbrecht (USA) at the 1992 Winter Games.

• The first skier to win three medals in Olympic moguls competition is Kari Traa (NOR), who won bronze in 1998, gold in 2002, and then silver in 2006. No other skier has captured this many medals in Olympic freestyle competition.

• In the 2002 Olympics, Jennifer Heil (CAN) missed the bronze medal by one-hundredth of a point! Four years later, in 2006, she dominated the moguls competition and claimed the gold medal.

EQUIPMENT TIPS

To help them do their tricks, freestyle skiers use shorter skis than alpine skiers, as well as longer, stronger poles.

Canada's Jennifer Heil goes for the gold in the 2006 moguls event.

SKI CROSS

Ski cross combines the speed of downhill skiing, the technical jumps of moguls, and the frenzy of a crowd of skiers racing across the snow at once.

Ski cross competitors at the 2009 World Championships.

THIS IS A NEW EVENT, SO NO OLYMPIC RECORDS EXIST.

NEW KID ON THE BLOCK

Ski cross is the newest Olympic freestyle event, making its debut at the 2010 Olympics. Ski cross races are fast and exciting. The unpredictable outcome and possibility of collisions make this a dangerous but thrill-packed sport!

RACE BASICS

Skiers are divided into groups of four. Each group competes together in two **heats**, or races. A skier's times are added together, and the two skiers with the fastest times advance to the next round. There are several heats leading up to the final race, which is called the Big Final.

SKI CROSS COURSE

A variety of obstacles are spread along the course, including jumps, turns, bumps, and flat sections. Skiers navigate the course at speeds of up to 43 MPH (70 km/h)!

DID YOU KNOW?

- Passing other skiers to get ahead is the name of the game in ski cross! Passing zones are flat areas where skiers are allowed to pass.

- Skiers who interfere with other competitors by pushing, pulling, holding, or blocking are disqualified.

- A ski cross race lasts only about 60 seconds from start to finish.

BACKGROUND TRAINING

Most competitors in ski cross have a background in alpine skiing, which gives them some of the racing skills needed in this challenging event.

A RELATIVE OF SNOWBOARD

Ski cross is similar to snowboard cross, which debuted at the 2006 Winter Olympics. The courses for the two events are very much alike, except that one sport is done on a snowboard while the other is done on skis.

START YOUR ENGINES!

Ski cross may be new to the Olympics, but it is not new to many extreme skiers. Ski cross is also known as Skier Cross or Skier-X in other international competitions. The sport has been compared to motocross—a **mass-start** race in which a group of competitors ride motorcycles over challenging obstacles.

A SNAPSHOT OF TH
VANCOUVER 2010
WINTER OLYMPICS

ALPINE AND FREESTYLE SKIING
THE ATHLETES

Everyone is getting ready for Vancouver in 2010! A new event added to the Vancouver Olympics is the sport of ski cross. Olympic teams are still being determined. The listings below include the top finishers in a selection of events in the 2009 World Cup and the 2009 FIS Freestyle World Ski Championships. Who among them will be the athletes to watch in the Vancouver Winter Olympics? Visit the Web site www.vancouver2010.com for more information about the upcoming competitions.

The sport of ski cross has been added as an official event at the Vancouver Olympics. The mass start of skiers and varied terrain of the course make this an exciting competition.

ALPINE EVENTS

Men — Downhill:
1. Michael Walchhofer (AUT)
2. Klaus Kroll (AUT)
3. Didier Defago (SUI)
4. Askel Lund Svindal (NOR)
5. Manuel Osborne-Paradis (CAN)

Men — Super G:
1. Askel Lund Svindal (NOR)
2. Werner Heel (ITA)
3. Didier Defago (SUI)
4. Hermann Maier (AUT)
5. Christof Innerhofer (ITA)

Men — Giant Slalom:
1. Didier Cuche (SUI)
2. Benjamin Raich (AUT)
3. Ted Ligety (USA)
4. Massimiliano Blardone (ITA)
5. Askel Lund Svindal (NOR)

Women — Downhill:
1. Lindsey Vonn (USA)
2. Andrea Fischbacher (AUT)
3. Maria Riesch (GER)
4. Dominique Gisin (SUI)
5. Nadia Fanchini (ITA)

Women — Super G:
1. Lindsey Vonn (USA)
2. Nadia Fanchini (ITA)
3. Fabienne Suter (SUI)
4. Anja Parson (SWE)
5. Andrea Dettling (SUI)

Women — Giant Slalom:
1. Tanja Poutiainen (FIN)
2. Kathrin Zettel (AUT)
3. Tina Maze (SLO)
4. Elisabeth Gorgl (AUT)
5. Denise Karbon (ITA)

FREESTYLE EVENTS

Men — Ski Cross:
1. Andreas Matt (AUT)
2. Thomas Zangerl (AUT)
3. Davey Barr (CAN)

Men — Moguls:
1. Patrick Deneen (USA)
2. Tapio Luusua (FIN)
3. Vincent Marquis (CAN)

Men — Aerials:
1. Ryan St. Onge (USA)
2. Steve Omiscl (CAN)
3. Warren Shouldice (CAN)

Women — Ski Cross:
1. Ashleigh McIvor (CAN)
2. Karin Huttary (AUT)
3. Meryll Boulangeat (AUT)

Women — Moguls:
1. Aiko Uemura (JPN)
2. Jennifer Heil (CAN)
3. Nikola Sudova (CZE)

Women — Aerials:
1. Li Nina (CHN)
2. Xu Mengato (CHN)
3. Jacqui Cooper (AUS)

THE VENUES IN VANCOUVER

ALPINE SKIING
WHISTLER CREEKSIDE

- venue capacity: 7,600
- located in Whistler, British Columbia
- regularly hosts International Ski Federation (FIS) World Cup competitions
- men's alpine skiing events on the Dave Murray Downhill
- women's alpine skiing events on Franz's Run
- finish area elevation: 2,657 feet (810 m)

FREESTYLE SKIING
CYPRESS MOUNTAIN

- venue capacity: 8000
- located in Cypress Provincial Park, overlooking the city of Vancouver
- elevation: 3051 feet (930 m)

Cypress mountain

29

GLOSSARY

aerodynamic Designed to move without being blocked by the wind

air bump A jump that has been constructed on a moguls course

breakaway gate A gate designed to return to position after being knocked

compacted Pressed down so it takes up very little space

debut To perform something for the first time or the first time an event is added to competition

degree of difficulty A set score for rating moves that is taken into account in the overall score

demonstration sport A sport that is played at the Olympics on a trial basis

disqualified To be eliminated from competition for not following the rules

heat One run down a course in a competition

hinge A movable joint that makes it possible for something to bend one way, then bend back into position

inverted Turned upside down

kicker A snow-covered ramp that aerial skiers use to launch themselves into the air

margin of victory The difference in time or score between a first-place finish and the second-place finish

mass-start A race format in which several athletes begin at once

mogul A bump on a ski course

podium A platform on which the winners of an event stand

qualifying round A stage of competition that competitors must succeed at in order to move on to the next stage

tiara A crown covered with jewels

wind resistance A force created by air that resists the movement of something that is going forward

FIND OUT MORE

BOOKS

Deutsch, Jessica. *Downhill Skiing for Fun!* (Minneapolis: Compass Point Books, 2009)

Herran, Joe, and Ron Thomas. *Skiing* (Philadelphia: Chelsea House, 2007)

Judd, Ron C. *The Winter Olympics: An Insider's Guide to the Legends, the Lore, and the Games* (Seattle: Mountaineers Books, 2009)

MacAulay, Kelley, and Bobbie Kalman. *Extreme Skiing* (St. Catharines, Ontario: Crabtree Publishing, 2006)

Schindler, John E. *Extreme Skiing* (Milwaukee: Gareth Stevens, 2005)

Smith, Warren. *Go Ski* (New York: Dorling Kindersley, 2006)

WEB SITES

Alpine Canada Alpin (ACA)   www.canski.org
The site of the governing body for ski racing in Canada.

Canadian Olympic Committee   www.olympic.ca
The official site of the Canadian Olympic Committee, with information on athletes, sports, and the Olympics.

International Olympic Committee   www.olympic.org
The official site of the International Olympic Committee, with information on all Olympic sports.

International Ski Federation (FIS)   www.fis-ski.com
The official site of the organization, made up of more than 100 national ski federations, overseeing all types of competitive skiing.

U.S. Olympic Committee   www.usoc.org/
The official site of the U.S. Olympic Committee, with information on athletes, sports, and the Olympics.

U.S. Ski Team   www.usskiteam.com
The official site of the U.S. teams in all types of skiing.

INDEX

COUNTRY ABBREVIATIONS

Printed in the U.S.A. — CG